# The Complete
# Shadow
# Workbook & Journal

## G. Noble

# The Complete Shadow Workbook & Journal

## Disclaimer:

The information contained in this book is meant for educational purposes only and is not intended to diagnose, treat, cure, or prevent any illness or condition. You acknowledge that this book is not a substitute for professional consultation with a certified practitioner. Consult your own physician or healthcare professional regarding the suggestions and advice contained in this book. Acceptance of this disclaimer is implied by your use of this book.

The publisher and author make no assurances about the amount of success you will experience as a consequence of implementing the advice and tactics included in this book, and you accept the risk that individual outcomes may vary. In addition, the publisher and the author assume no responsibility for errors, inaccuracies, omissions, or any other inconsistencies herein.

Content Source: shape.com, healthline.com, mindbodygreen.com, scottjeffrey.com

Published By: Unicorn Publishers
Copyright © 2021 G. Noble.

First Printing Edition 2021.

"Until you make the unconscious conscious, it will direct your life and you will call it fate."

— C.G. Jung

# FOREWORD

While you almost certainly have a dark side — according to psychology, everyone has — there is also a technique that may help you move through that aspect of yourself. It's called "shadow work," and according to therapist Akua Boateng, Ph.D., it entails "dive[ing] into the unconscious stuff that determines our ideas, feelings, and actions." The idea is to bring such unconscious fixations — such as the anguish associated with a traumatic incident — into conscious consciousness so that they may be addressed in treatment, according to Boateng. These unconscious parts, which are responsible for your impulsive acts and comprise a portion of your so-called dark side, might be triggered by traumatic events, trauma, or old memories, Boateng adds.

Boateng asserts that confronting one's history is crucial for recovery. "As a result, I advise clients to develop a new connection with some of their psyche's unlikeable, irrational, and wounded elements in order to incorporate new patterns into their life," she continues. This is when shadow work enters the picture.

# How Is Shadow Work Defined?

The term "shadow self" was popularized by Swiss psychiatrist Carl Jung, M.D. It refers to a half of yourself that you may have learnt to repress as a kid. For instance, if you were reprimanded for throwing a tantrum, you may have suppressed your anger and presented the world with a more socially acceptable smiling face. You were taught from an early age that anger was unwelcome. This fury, along with rage, envy, greed, and self-centeredness, are universal emotions that not everyone feels comfortable expressing. These suppressed emotions or features are considered to be a component of your shadow personality.

"Shadow work is all about the unconscious mind," explains Danielle Massi, L.M.F.T. "It's about the things we repress and conceal from ourselves, such as traumas and shadow personas." Your shadow self may manifest when you are provoked, in your relationships, or when you are experiencing varied degrees of anxiety and sadness, she explains. And if this supposedly evil side does emerge, it may suggest something about your personality that is worth investigating further.

While anybody may perform shadow work, a qualified mental health professional is the greatest choice for therapy, particularly for someone who has suffered serious trauma, such as surviving an accident or seeing violence or abuse. That's because, according to the Center for Health Care Strategies, they're educated to assist you in working through trauma without re-traumatizing you, or generating further emotional and biological stress. Massi has regularly conducted shadow work with many of her clients over the last year. "For a decade as a psychotherapist, I felt that my clients and I could only go so far in our explorations of the conscious and subconscious minds," she explains. "In order to best assist my clients, I transitioned from standard psychotherapy to shadow work in order to assist them in healing on a much deeper level."

# How The Shadow Is Created

Each small kid is aware of compassion, love, and charity, but also of rage, selfishness, and greed.

These emotions are an integral element of our common humanity. However, as we mature, something occurs. Accepted are characteristics connected with "being good," whereas those associated with "being bad" are rejected. Every human being has basic human requirements. These include physiological requirements, safety and security requirements, and a need for belonging. These are biological and instinctive demands.

When we were youngsters, we received negative indications from our surroundings when we expressed certain aspects of ourselves. Perhaps we were enraged and threw a tantrum. Our parents chastised us for our outburst and escorted us to our room.

Alternatively, we may have acted audaciously, playfully, impulsively, or foolishly in our first-grade classroom. Our teacher chastised us in front of the class for our lack of etiquette and urged us to sit down.

Whenever that occurred — and it may have occurred frequently — it jeopardized one of our most fundamental requirements. Would our parents' disapproval jeopardize our safety? Would our professors' and classmates' condemnation undermine our urge to belong? We shaped our behavior to meet our requirements and developed the ability to adapt to the external world.

All of the pieces of us that are unaccepted or discouraged over the first two decades of our life get bundled up and swept out of view (outside our conscious awareness). As poet Robert Bly describes in A Little Book of the Human Shadow, the youngster collects all of these undesirable pieces and drags them behind him in an unseen bag. This repression of undesirable aspects results in the formation of what psychologist Carl Jung referred to as the personal shadow.

# Isn't It True That We All Have A Shadow?

In a word, yeah. According to licensed therapist and co-founder of Viva Wellness Jor-El Caraballo, LMHC, the lengthy response is as follows: Yes, however you may hear it referred to by another name.

"While the idea of the shadow is commonly acknowledged in analytical psychology," he explains, it is far from the sole perspective on the human mind. Shadow work can also be classified as self-reflection, self-examination, or similar terms.

Whatever you name it, "the majority of therapists are tasked with the responsibility of assisting clients in making the unconscious conscious, which is a central component of shadow work," Caraballo notes. "As a therapist, I believe that we all have a shadow aspect that, when integrated, may be well-accepted and help us manage our own mental health and relationships more effectively."

# The Objective Of Shadow Work

"Through shadow work, I've witnessed people break habits of self-sabotage, addiction, and codependency," Boateng explains. "Some have been confronted with subconscious tendencies resulting from childhood sexual, physical, or psychological abuse. By confronting the shadow that you were previously fighting, you might gain insight into how your ideas and feelings impact your behavior and shape your reality. By accepting responsibility for your projections, you empower yourself."

Many persons who engage in shadow labor do it in order to "ascertain why." This entails tracing the origins of their patterns, which, according to Boateng, contribute to their shadow selves. "Rather than withdrawing from taught behavior, leaning in with empathy results in dramatic change," Boateng explains. "We all have a natural desire to adapt to our surroundings, and occasionally those circumstances demand us to take unfavorable actions to defend ourselves." Translation: Frequently, your answers are motivated by self-preservation. For example, shutting down emotionally throughout childhood may have served you well, but it may have harmed your relationships in the future.

# The Advantages Of Shadowing

Among the advantages of shadowing are the following:

- A Sense Of Completeness Or Integration As A Person.
- Enhanced Interpersonal Relationships.
- Resolving Ancestral Trauma.
- Acquiring Skills For Meeting Your Needs In A Healthy Manner.

## YOU MAY HAVE A SENSE OF COMPLETENESS.

Although there is no peer-reviewed research on shadow work, Short asserts that it can help you gain a more comprehensive perspective on yourself.

"A lot of individuals speak in fragments about themselves," Short observes. "When I work with clients on their 'parts', it is to assist them see that they can and have always been entire, but that their previous experiences caused them to feel fragmented."

## IT MAY HAVE AN EFFECT ON HOW YOU INTERACT WITH PEOPLE

Short asserts that as you increase your self-awareness, you will come to trust yourself more. Additionally, you may apply this reflection to relationships.

For instance, perhaps you were admonished as a youngster not to "speak back" and now have difficulty standing up for yourself as an adult.

"By engaging in shadow work, you may establish boundaries and learn to speak your truth," Short explains.

## YOU MIGHT BE ABLE TO REPAIR GENERATIONAL TRAUMA

Shadow work has the potential to heal scars from childhood, which are frequently caused by primary caregivers such as a parent.

"You are always mending yourself, your parents, and the lineage, even more so when you begin to address generational traumas inside the shadow experience," Short explains.

Additionally, it might assist you in considering your approach to caring, should you have children.

"It forces you to examine your family structure and asks, 'Is this something I want to continue doing with my family?'" Short explains.

## YOU'LL BE ABLE TO SATISFY YOUR REQUIREMENTS IN A MORE HEALTHY MANNER

According to Sweeton, our shadow self can manifest detrimental actions. For example, those who have been taught that desiring to be close to someone is "clingy" may experience difficulties in future relationships and may cheat on a spouse.

Investigating one's shadow can assist individuals in developing more productive behaviors.

"When you are not concealing anything from yourself and can see yourself completely, it becomes much simpler to be in charge of yourself," Sweeton explains.

## INTUITIONAL TAPPING

Depending on what you've tucked away in your own shadow, there's a high possibility shadow work will assist you in connecting with your inner knowing or intuition. If you were discouraged as a youngster from trusting your gut and inner compass, Swat adds, "then you cast that into the shade."

## SELF-EMANCIPATION FROM THE UNCONSCIOUS SHADOW

When we are unconscious, our shadow successfully dominates us. Thus, while confronting our shadow is challenging, it is also extremely liberating. "It all sounds very bad," Swart explains, "but it's critical to bring it from unconscious to awareness, because then it can't govern you the way it does when it remains suppressed."

## SELF-EMPOWERMENT AND ACCEPTANCE OF ONE'S STRENGTHS

"Intriguingly, people with extremely low self-esteem frequently bury positive aspects of themselves in their shadows because they don't feel deserving," Swart adds. In such cases, shadow work enables us to recover the gifts that define us and have been hidden away.

## TAKING A STEP FORWARD IN THE DIRECTION OF SELF-ACTUALIZATION

If you're interested in shadow work, you're probably also interested in personal development and progress. And, as Swart asserts, shadow labor is vital for everyone seeking fulfillment and self-actualization. "In order to become the best version of yourself, you must first identify the negative aspects of yourself that are holding you back or are concealed," she explains.

Bear in mind the following when performing shadow work:

## BE AWARE OF YOUR TRIGGERS

To paraphrase Jung, "Everything that bothers us about others might help us understand ourselves." As you progress through this training, you'll gain an increasing awareness of the small things that trigger you—and why. As a result, keep an eye out.

"If there is something you've always desired and you see a buddy doing it," Swart explains, "that creates shadows, because it's as if you're wondering why that person has it and I don't."

## ALLOW YOURSELF TO BE GRACIOUS

Shadow work is not easy, and it is critical to extend compassion to those aspects of ourselves that have been buried for so long.

"Many individuals put off that task out of fear of what they may discover," Swart adds. "There is a great deal of guilt involved with these issues [...], but if you are mature or personally evolved enough, performing shadow work may be a wonderful relief because you discover it is not as horrible as you believe."

## SOLICIT ASSISTANCE FROM OTHERS.

Again, shadow work is never easy—even more so if you have experienced trauma. If contemplating your shadow selves results in anguish, sorrow, or dread that you feel unprepared to deal, it's time to seek the assistance of a competent expert.

"I believe it is critical for anyone engaged in shadow work to have items that assist them in feeling anchored and accepted," Caraballo observes. "While a nonjudgmental therapist may assist tremendously, we also need our own skills to help us reaffirm and embrace ourselves when we confront our most challenging feelings and aspects."

There are several approaches to this, depending on your tastes, with Caraballo suggesting grounding exercises, affirmations, and therapeutic writing.

# Repression In The Shadows

Maintaining a concealed shadow is a sort of repression, and specialists warn that it may have negative implications.

"It's similar to knowing that you have a problem but not allowing yourself to address it fully," Short explains.

### Individuals May:

- Self-Soothe With Drugs Or Alcohol.
- Speak Poorly About Themselves.
- Feel Stress.
- Struggle With Mental Health Issues Such As Depression Or Anxiety.

"Instead of facing what's causing you anguish," Short explains, "you take your pain out on yourself."

According to Sweeton, suppressing a shadow can lead to individuals living inauthentic lifestyles.

"People struggle with self-identity and communicating what matters to them and what they value," she explains. "This can cause people to make poor job or relationship choices, but they have difficulty realizing why."

# How To Perform Shadow Work Effectively

Carl Jung, a Swiss psychiatrist and psychotherapist, popularized shadow work in Western society, according to Jennifer Sweeton, PsyD, MS, MA, a licensed clinical psychologist and owner of Mind Works Consulting and Psychological Services, PLLC.

"[Shadow work] is the concept that everyone of us possesses distinct aspects of ourselves," Sweeton explains. "The aspects of ourselves that have been banished... inevitably become shadow selves."

According to Djuan Short, LCSW, RYT-500, a holistic certified clinical social worker at Dahlia Rose Wellness, everyone has a shadow that often manifests throughout infancy.

"As a youngster, you are frequently instructed to cease doing something... or to repress aspects of yourself that have been considered unsuitable for whatever reason," Short explains.

According to experts, investigating shadows can yield critical information.

"Through this practice, you're attempting to develop a stronger connection to yourself and your soul in order to become a more full version of yourself," Sweeton explains.

Prior to beginning shadow work, there are a few points to consider.

## WHAT NOVICES SHOULD BE AWARE OF

According to Sweeton, patients do not automatically begin shadowing. It takes time, and novices must cultivate a greater awareness of feelings they may dismiss otherwise.

"You're going to have to be deliberate in observing your own reactions," Sweeton explains. "Someone who has done this for a long period of time will be more proficient at it."

Sweeton proposes that those new to shadow work keep a running journal of times they experience intense emotions and the circumstances around them. According to her, symptoms include the sensation of a "gut punch" or a constriction of the chest.

"The shadow is most visible at times of intense emotion," she explains. "Keeping track of the emotions... and sensations that you experience might assist you in identifying patterns."

# A Comprehensive Guide To Shadowing

Shadow labor, according to Short, is like to peeling back the layers of an onion.

"Consider instances when you sense something bubbling within you and you're unsure why you're so unhappy," Short explains. "You're unhappy because a part of you has been hiding for a long time... and is now ready to come out."

Sweeton asserts that it is critical to pause and think on these situations rather than accepting things at face value and moving on.

"Oftentimes, when we hear or see something, we instantly evaluate it and turn it off," Sweeton explains. "By judging oneself, you alienate yourself. The analysis then comes to an end, and we carry on with our lives. I want individuals to be aware of their powerful feelings and to accept them."

# Test Of Shadow Work

Short offers the following five questions to ponder before to beginning shadow work:

1. What is my identity?
2. What am I seeking?
3. What am I willing to give up in order to obtain the things I desire?
4. What am I required to become in order to acquire those things?
5. How do I wish to present myself?

# Inquiring About Shadow Work in Therapy

To assess if you should pursue shadow work, Boateng suggests observing your interpersonal dynamics and, more especially, any patterns in which you tend to become trapped (i.e. calling off a good "thing" the moment a potential partner starts to open up and wants you to do the same.) And if you decide to give this sort of treatment a try, Massi suggests "collaborating with a therapist versed in shadow work." That individual may have completed certified courses and earned a Complementary Medicine Association-recognized Shadow Mastery Diploma.

A competent therapist may start a shadow work session by helping you to reach a meditative state — as Massi does with her patients by asking them to relax and breathe deeply. "When we are active and away from home, we are in a beta brain wave condition," Massi adds. "We are in a theta [state] while we are falling asleep. We are also in a theta state while we are in a meditative state. Thus, a good approach to think about being in a meditative state is to imagine yourself as you slip off to sleep; alert and aware, yet little sleepy due to the brain waves' decreased frequency." This places you in a state of consciousness that is not your own.

Massi employs certain lines of questioning to assist her clients retrieve suppressed memories after bringing them into a fully peaceful state. She urges students to engage "all of their senses to ensure that the information comes through vividly — since memories are encoded using many senses — and then I let them take the lead," she explains. "I invite people to share their experiences [when accessing a memory], and I just guide them through the process," by probing further into the memory with questions.

Does this sound familiar? Perhaps your therapist is already using some aspects of shadow work into your treatment. "Some therapists may classify it as 'self-awareness work' or 'emotional intelligence,'" Boateng explains. "Frequently, psychoanalytic or psychodynamically educated practitioners [therapists or psychiatrists] use shadow work," but they do it in conjunction with other modalities of therapy, such as attachment and trauma-based work.

Unfortunately, there is no directory of practitioners who specialize in shadow work, and according to Massi, it is still regarded a "new age" spiritual activity. However, the Psychology Today therapist database allows you to search for Jungian-style therapy, which is a larger technique of integrating the conscious and unconscious minds, and from there, you may query about shadow work. Additionally, conducting a Google search for "shadow employment near me" may be beneficial.

# Attempting Shadow Work Independently

Though it is recommended to begin with a therapist, many people prefer to perform shadow work on their own, according to Boateng.

Jenny Sarah, 32, of Milwaukee, is through a transforming experience with shadow work as a result of her own research and application. "I believe it's worth the work to have a better understanding of some of the unhealthy decisions I've made — particularly in relationships," Sarah tells Shape. "I've realized that through time, I've developed a tendency to attempt to 'fix' my significant others, even when they don't require or want it." She feels that her tendency to be a "fixer" stems from her childhood.

To begin your personal practice, Massi recommends "starting with meditation." "When we meditation, our thoughts relax into an altered brain state that facilitates access to the unconscious mind." (Related: The Meditation Beginner's Guide)

Massi suggests attempting to relax for at least five minutes by listening to peaceful music and looking at a lighted candle. She advises observing your mind's wanderings and keeping a log of your experiences and any unpleasant ideas that arise. "Rather of attempting to push things out of your head, welcome them in," she advises. These ideas can be illuminating, as Massi argues. Inquire as to what your thoughts are communicating, since this can aid in the discovery of your shadow self.

Additionally, it's worthwhile to consider what triggers you on a regular basis and why. According to Boateng, a smart place to start is by observing relationship dynamics. "Are you prone to become enraged during specific sorts of conversations? Or are you depressed when you watch others succeed? These are internal emotions that convey a tale about your previous experiences "she asserts. Massi has also produced a shadow work diary, which you can purchase online. The journal has shadow work prompts that can assist you in delving deeper into your darkness.

As is the case with all types of therapy and self-reflection, shadow work requires time and purpose, and can be difficult at times. It's critical to approach the procedure with self-compassion, according to Boateng. "Rather of judging ourselves for our actions, we must hold ourselves accountable for our recovery from the event."

# Experiments In Shadow Work

The following activities will assist you in developing your shadow work in and out of the treatment session.

## CONSIDER INSTANCES WHEN YOU WENT TOO FAR.

According to Short, examining areas of your life where you overextend yourself, such as working late hours, reveals how you interact with yourself and others.

"This also gives you a general idea of which topics you may want to examine more and focus on," Short adds.

### Consider it:

- Consider the following: What do I overdo?
- Create a list of your replies.
- Consider why. What are your objectives? What chasm are you attempting to bridge?
- Make a list of these replies.

## DEFICIENCIES VS. ENHANCEMENTS

According to Short, this practice can assist you in gaining a better understanding of how your daily events affect you

### Consider it:

- Take a blank sheet of paper and divide it into two columns.
- "Depletes Me" is the subject of Column A. Column B is titled "Improves My Position."
- Consider the encounters that impede your progress. They should be listed in column A.
- Consider encounters that bring you joy. They should be listed in column B.

## DECLARE IT ALOUD

According to Sweeton, admitting shadow aspects of oneself to a loved one or therapist might help with self-acceptance and minimize feelings of shame.

### Consider it:

- Identify possible shadow roles.

- With a friend or therapist, discuss the shadow aspect and how it may have arisen. "For instance, you may say, 'I want to be protected, yet I've been taught that's a sign of weakness,'" Sweeton explains.
- Discuss how this reality affects your life and how you may control the negative aspects.

## REVERSE THE SCRIPT

According to Sweeton, shadow parts frequently have a bad connotation — but they shouldn't.

"All characteristics and roles, including shadow roles, have a positive," she explains. "Once you've identified your shadow parts, consider the potential benefits of the shadow part."

### **Consider it:**

- Recognize possible shadow characters, such as impostor syndrome.
- Consider and identify the ways in which your shadow selves assist you. "If you have a shadow self that fears incompetence, the positive may be that you are meticulous, self-aware, and scrupulous," Sweeton adds.
- Remind yourself of these good characteristics, particularly when perceived negative characteristics surface.

## DETERMINE WORTH

While shadow portions might be disturbing, Sweeton adds that they can also show our ideals.

### __Consider it:__

- Create a list of shadow parts.
- Consider what these sections reveal about your personal ideals.
- Consider strategies to live in accordance with your values.

## CONSIDER SOMEONE WHO IRRITATES YOU

"One way the shadow manifests itself for us is through what we find most repulsive or challenging in others," Caraballo explains. "Frequently, these pictures are a mirror of aspects of ourselves we find repulsive."

Thus, a good place to begin with shadow work is to consider someone who irritates you and concentrate on what it is about that person that may be present within you, he adds. To ascertain this, he suggests that you ask yourself kind questions such as:

- What is it about this individual that I dislike?
- Do I occasionally exhibit any of those similar characteristics?
- What makes being with them so difficult?
- What aspects of myself do they revitalize when I'm with them? And what is my attitude toward that aspect of myself?

## TAKE A LOOK AT YOUR FAMILY TREE.

Swart presents another introductory activity for dipping your toes into shadow work: family tree analysis.

"Create a family tree for your two sets of grandparents, all of your aunts and uncles, and your parents," she continues. "These are the generations above you whose characteristics—both good and bad—might be present in you." This exercise is all about developing the courage to declare, "I like my family, but one of my uncles drinks excessively," as Swart illustrates.

The next stage is to examine all of the characteristics that exist within your family and determine whether any of them exist inside you.

## FACE YOUR DARKNESS

Another activity is contemplating and facing one's own shadow. Once you have a clear (or at least reasonably clear) picture of the components of your shadow self, you may begin facing and releasing them using positive affirmations such as:

- I release the deepest shadow that has been dormant within me.
- I let go of fear; I let go of uncertainty; I let go of embarrassment; I let go of insecurity.

## KEEP AN EYE ON YOUR EMOTIONAL REACTIONS

Bear in mind that the shadow is elusive; it conceals itself behind us. Our defensive systems are programmed to keep our shadows hidden and unseen.

The more conscious you are of your actions and emotions, the more likely you are to catch your shadow in the act.

We have a tendency to project our disowned selves onto others.

One of the most effective methods for identifying your shadow is to monitor your emotional reactions to other individuals.

While your coworkers may be aggressive, arrogant, inconsiderate, or impatient, if you lack similar characteristics, you will not respond strongly to their conduct.

If you're vigilant, you may teach yourself to recognize your shadow when you observe others exhibit significant negative emotional responses.

As Jung is frequently cited as saying:

Everything that frustrates us about others might point us in the direction of self-awareness.

However, we rarely have the opportunity to engage with such feelings in the moment.

At the end of the day, taking five or ten minutes to reflect on your contacts with others and your subsequent emotions is beneficial.

What irritates you in another person is almost always an unacknowledged aspect of yourself.

Acquaint yourself with that aspect, embrace it, and integrate it into your being, and the next time you witness it in someone, it may not elicit such powerful emotional responses.

Concentrate on what and people elicit an emotional response in you. It makes no difference what feeling you are experiencing; it is a sign that you are rejecting something within you.

## ENGAGE IN SELF-DISCUSSION

Numerous sorts of inner work necessitate an active interaction with your shadow self.

At first glance, this may appear to be a frightening concept, given our widespread perception that only "mad people" communicate with themselves. However, each of us has countless subpersonalities—numerous unseen, independent aspects of our mind.

Numerous psychologies include Jung's Active Imagination, Schwartz's Internal Family Systems, Stone and Winkleman's Voice Dialogue, and Assagioli's Psychosynthesis as approaches to coping with these divergent elements.

When we ignore these elements — which may or may not reflect facets of our shadow — they have a way of affecting our behavior.

Have you ever done or said anything and then questioned your actions or words? A part of you was seizing control.

Each ostensibly "accident" is a component of your behavior being hijacked.

Our disowned parts do not intend to cause us harm, yet they frequently do when we ignore or deny them.

We may incorporate these components into our conscious selves by conversing with them in our imagination or in a diary.

Then they become our allies rather than our adversaries.

## CONFRONT THE POSITIVE ASPECT

Many of us consider ourselves to be "nice people." As youngsters, we were complimented for being a "good boy" or "good girl," and that label lingered with us.

This exacerbated the schism between our aware and shadow selves.

Create a list of all your positive characteristics. Then emphasize the polar opposite. Make an attempt to locate the polar opposite within yourself.

For instance, if you identify yourself as a disciplined individual, you are repressing your slothful side. The slothful component is concealing itself in the shadows.

The disowned is continually interfering with your conduct and challenging your disciplined self.

As such, identify with this slothful aspect. Observe it. Acknowledge it. Make it a buddy. It's OK to be slothful as well.

## DISCOVER THE SHADOW ARCHETYPES

Perhaps the most effective approach to become acquainted with your shadow is to become acquainted with the writings of neo-Jungian Robert Moore.

Moore asserts that the King, Warrior, Magician, and Lover are the four fundamental archetypes of the mind.

Each archetype embodies what we consider to be the greatest characteristics of mature adulthood.

However, for every constructive archetype, there is a corresponding negative counterpart.

And not one, but two shadows: an active side and a passive side (bipolar).

For instance, the Tyrant and the Weakling are the King's shadows. The Sadist and Masochist are the Warrior's shadows.

Acquainting oneself with these bipolar shadows enables you to recognize their thinking and behavioral patterns inside yourself.

Moore and Gillette's King, Warrior, Magician, and Lover are highly recommended. It's one of the most significant psychological books I've ever read.

# The Shadow Process of 3-2-1

If you're looking for a step-by-step strategy for working with your shadow, check out Ken Wilber's 3-2-1 Shadow Process in Integral Life Practice.

## The Following Are The Fundamental Steps:

**Step 1: Decide on a medium to work with:**
It's frequently simpler to begin with someone with whom you're having problems (e.g., partner, relative, boss).

This individual may irritate, bother, or upset you. Alternatively, you may be drawn to, obsessed with, fascinated with, or possessive of this somebody.

Choose someone who evokes powerful emotional responses in you, whether favorable or negative.

**Step 2: Confront it:** Now consider this individual. Using third-person language, describe the attributes that most irritate you or the characteristics that most appeal you (he, she, it).

Discuss them aloud or in a diary. Communicate your emotions.

Don't overcomplicate it; simply express what has to be said. There is no reason to be courteous. The individual you describe will never see this.

**Step 3: Communicate with it:** In your mind, have a conversation with this individual. Address this individual in the second person (using the "you" language).

Communicate directly with this individual as though he or she were present. Inform them of what irritates you about them.

Inquire of them the following:

- Why, Why are you torturing me?
- What do you require of me?
- What are you attempting to demonstrate to me?
- What are you attempting to educate me?

Consider their responses to these inquiries. Declare your fictitious reaction aloud. If you choose, you may record the talk in your diary.

**Step 4: Become it:** Take on the identity of this person. Take on the characteristics that irritate or attract you.

Take on the characteristics you mentioned in step 2. Employ first-person language ( I, me, mine).

This may be uncomfortable, and it should be. The characteristics you are adopting are precisely the characteristics you have been rejecting in yourself.

Utilize Assertions Such As:
- I am enraged.
- I am envious.
- I am ethereal.
- "I am ."

**Step 5:** Become aware of these disowned characteristics within yourself.

Experiment with the aspect of yourself that embodies this feature. Avoid abstracting or conceptualizing the process; simply BE it.

Now is the time to reclaim and incorporate this characteristic inside yourself.

## HOW MUCH TIME DOES SHADOW WORK REQUIRE?

As with many other facets of mental health work, shadowing can take time. Each individual is unique.

"If there was childhood [trauma], it will be more difficult and may take several years to get to the shadow stage of treatment," Sweeton explains. "If someone comes in with a relatively trauma-free past but does have some sadness or anxiety, it may take many months to treat and resolve it."

Even after addressing and resolving one aspect of your history, Short asserts that shadow work is a never-ending path.

"You develop an ability to integrate the many components of digesting it throughout your life," she explains.

## SHADOW LABOR HAS A SPIRITUAL DIMENSION

For some, shadow labor might seem like soul care, which Sweeton believes benefits individuals in your immediate vicinity.

"By connecting with yourself and your soul, you may access portions of yourself that you cannot see, which may enable you to feel a broader spectrum of emotions that can be used to improve yourself and others," Sweeton explains.

For instance, Sweeton asserts that confronting your anger rather than rejecting it might lead you down a road toward channeling your energy into opposing injustice.

"You may channel your rage in a more constructive manner to effect positive change in the world," Sweeton adds.

According to some therapists, the insights gained via shadow work may even seem spiritual.

## IS SHADOW WORK RISKY?

Sweeton asserts that anybody may profit from shadow labor and that avoiding it is actually riskier.

"There is nothing about you that is intolerable," Sweeton constantly tells her clients. "Whatever is going on inside of you is already manifesting itself. Having a look at it makes it safer."

Nonetheless, it is suggested that you engage in shadow work with the assistance of a qualified therapist.

# Five Positive Consequences of Jungian Shadow Work

The shadow is not a well-liked subject.

Who appreciates being accountable for their flaws, inadequacies, selfishness, rudeness, and hatred, to name a few?

Concentrating on our abilities is more fun and affirming of our lives. However, examining our shadow side provides us with enormous potential for growth and development.

Consider the following five benefits of Jungian shadow work:

## 1) STRENGTHENED RELATIONSHIPS

As you integrate your shadow side and reconcile with your darker half, you gain a clearer view of yourself. You develop a stronger sense of self-awareness, humanity, and wholeness.

Accepting one's own darkness makes it simpler to accept the shadow in others.

As a consequence, you will be less easily triggered by other people's actions. Additionally, you'll find it easier to communicate with people.

Your connections with your spouse, family members, friends, and business partners may improve.

## 7) IMPROVED PERCEPTION

By accepting others and yourself as they are, you may view the world through a clearer lens.

By integrating your shadow self, you're bringing yourself closer to your actual self, which provides a more accurate appraisal of who you are.

You will not regard oneself as being too large (inflated) or excessively little (deflated).

When you are self-aware, you can make more accurate assessments of your environment.

You'll perceive persons and circumstances more clearly, compassionately, and understandingly.

## 2) INCREASED VITALITY AND PHYSICAL HEALTH

Dragging this phantom bag of belongings behind us is exhausting. It's tough effort to constantly deny and conceal all of the aspects of ourselves that we'd rather avoid confronting in maturity.

Fatigue and lethargy are common afflictions of the unexamined life. Suppression of the mind can also result in bodily suffering and sickness.

Dr. John Sarno has aided hundreds of people suffering from chronic back pain in resolving their latent wrath.

Through Jungian shadow work, you may access a vast reserve of energy that you were unwittingly spending in self-protection.

This can have a beneficial effect on your physical, mental, and emotional wellbeing.

Shadow work may help you develop inner strength and a stronger sense of balance, preparing you to face life's obstacles.

## 4) INTEGRATION AND MATURITY OF THE PSYCHOLOGICAL SYSTEM

As long as we ignore our shadows and suppress some aspects of ourselves, we will struggle to achieve a sense of completeness and togetherness.

With a split mind, how can we have a feeling of completeness and balance?

Integrating the shadow takes you closer to experiencing a sense of completeness. It is a necessary step in attaining full maturity.

## 5) INCREASED IMAGINATION

One of the most significant benefits of Jungian shadow work is that it enables you to tap into more creative potential.

As psychologists such as Abraham Maslow and Carl Rogers discovered, creativity occurs spontaneously in psychologically healthy (integrated) persons.

# Five Suggestions When Engaging in Jungian Shadow Work

Here are five things that will make approaching your shadow easier:

## 1) ESTABLISH YOUR SELF-CENTERING

This is likely the most critical step before beginning shadow work. Despite this, working with the shadow is nearly never described in literature.

If you seek to become acquainted with your shadow self while you are not focused on your Self, you will receive no beneficial outcomes.

The shadow is a collection of disparate pieces buried within your psyche. You can only learn about these sections from your Center. If one of these components is "mixed" with you, the process will be hijacked.

You're going to be judgmental, critical, or perplexed. This will make it more difficult for you to incorporate your shadow.

You want to be in a quiet, clean, neutral area before you begin working with your shadow. That is, you desire to be a part of your Center.

## 7) DEVELOP SELF-COMPASSION

Prior to being acquainted with one's shadow, it is beneficial to build an unconditional goodwill for oneself. In Buddhism, it is referred to as Maitri.

Without self-compassion and kindness, it's tough to confront our darker aspects.

If you are harsh on yourself when you make errors, confronting your shadow will be challenging.

If you are used to experiencing shame or guilt, you must learn to replace these feelings with friendliness, self-acceptance, and self-compassion.

Begin by acknowledging your own humanity. Bear in mind that we all have a shadow—we are all in the same soup, as Jung used to say.

I find it beneficial to establish a connection with my heart: focus your attention on your heart. Take a deep breath and recognize your heart. Exhale and express gratitude to your heart. It is a straightforward Buddhist practice advocated by Thich Nhat Hanh.

## 3) DEVELOP SELF-AWARENESS

Seeing the shadow demands a self-reflective mindset—the capacity to watch and reflect on our actions, thoughts, and feelings.

Mindfulness meditation contributes to the development of nonjudgmental awareness—the capacity to be present in the moment without engaging the inner critic or other forms of judgment.

Self-awareness and self-reflection serve as a prelude to shadow work by enabling us to examine and assess our moods and emotional reactions without passing judgment or condemnation.

# 4) BE UNFLINCHINGLY HONEST

Self-awareness and integrity are necessary preconditions for shadow work.

While it's simple to give lip service to these virtues, genuine self-honesty requires us to be prepared to acknowledge the negative aspects of our conduct and personality.

Coming to grips with your disowned aspects is frequently painful, which is why the ego expends so much energy denying them.

Recognize and embrace your insecure selfishness and despotic evil aspects might be difficult.

It takes guts to examine your attitudes, habits, negative thoughts, and emotions honestly.

The benefits outweigh the agony, since these candid encounters with your shadow aid in the healing of mental divisions.

This bold deed expands your creative potential, creating new avenues for psychological development.

## 5) KEEP TRACK OF YOUR DISCOVERIES

I find it amazing how certain aspects of our disowned selves choose to stay hidden from our perspective.

Just like a dream may fade from memory minutes after awakening, our disowned pieces can do the same.

A writing notebook in which you chronicle your new self-discoveries is a treatment.

By recording your thoughts and evaluating them later, you can help encode the finding into your consciousness.

# The Shadow Workbook

# HOW YOU BEGIN

This workbook will navigate you through the darker regions of your consciousness, to be used in conjunction with a tarot or oracle deck, so at this time, select the tarot or oracle deck you will be using. The only specification for what type of deck to use is this: use one you have built a relationship with prior to this session, so that the deck can work expediently for you and is already pre-programmed to your personal energies.

At its core, this session is divination through cartomancy, but that divination is prompted by specific questions that challenge you to explore that which you might typically avoid. However, bear in mind that shadow work is a lifelong endeavor, with many facets. This workbook is by design limited in scope. It is only one self-guided session of shadow work.

Set aside one to two hours of quiet alone time. Begin by lighting incense or a scented candle that you know will bring you a sense of calm. Chamomile, lavender, sandalwood, jasmine, or vanilla are commonly used scents for calming, but use what works for you. In addition, you will need a bell, such as tingsha cymbals, a singing bowl, or any regular bell.

I also recommend that you light a larger pillar candle, one in a color and style that is most pleasing to you. To begin, after you have lit the incense or scented candle, light your pillar candle and envision the flame to be much larger than what the eyes can see. Imagine the spirit and aura of that flame encompassing all of you and your work space, protecting and shielding you. Invoke God, Spirit, your patron deities, angels, spirit guides, guardian spirits, or however you express divinity into the space and to fill you from within, to guide and shield you. Shuffle your deck and set it in front of you. Then begin the prompts of this workbook, filling the space allotted with your responses. Have a stack of loose leaf paper on hand in case you need extra pages for writing. Now let's begin.

When you were 11 to 13 years old, what was your dream? What did you envision yourself becoming? Describe exactly how 11- or 13-year-old you would have idealized yourself now, at your present age. Describe that idealized person you had wanted to be, the relationships you would have wanted in your life by now, the career or what you would be doing, and what you as that child expected ideally of you the adult. What did child-you expect the adult-you to have accomplished by now?

In what ways have you fallen short of that idealized vision you had of yourself back in childhood? What have you failed to achieve?

Shuffle your tarot or oracle deck and while you do so, reread what you wrote in the two earlier prompts. Reread it several times while you enter a meditative state and shuffle. Now you will be pulling three cards into the spread noted below. Before you pull each card, focus on the specific question presented for that card position. Write in your divinatory results into the card diagram. If symbols in the imagery stay with you, sketch them out into the card diagrams provided. These can be interpreted later as omens.

*Falling Short of Childhood Dreams...*

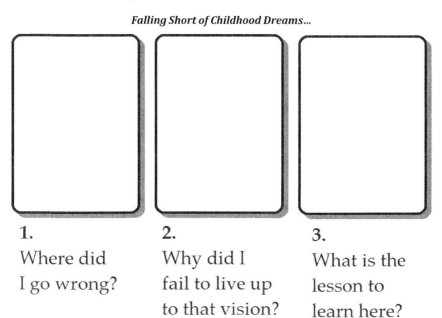

**1.**
Where did
I go wrong?

**2.**
Why did I
fail to live up
to that vision?

**3.**
What is the
lesson to
learn here?

After this session, return to the above divinatory reading and deep-dive into the messages of each card detail by detail, but for now, gaze upon the three cards and free-write your impressions below.

Page 53

What do you think your parents would have idealized you becoming? Do not get defensive and irrespective of your relationship (or lack thereof) with your parents, think about how this question would be answered if *your parents* were being candid and doing the shadow work. What were their highest expectations and idealized hopes for you?

How have you failed your parents? Again, do not get defensive and irrespective of what relationship you might have with them today, in *their* point of view, how might you have failed them? Disregard any impulse to defend yourself or your life choices. Let go of your defense mechanisms and think through their point of view, and the darkest, ugliest expression of that point of view.

How does your sense of falling short of parental expectations make you feel right now? Free-write on the emotions running through you at the moment.

Return to your tarot or oracle deck. Shuffle your deck and while you do so, reread what you wrote in the three earlier prompts. Then pull three cards into the spread below. Before you pull each card, focus on the specific question presented for that card position. Write in your divinatory results into the card diagram.

### *Falling Short of Parental Expectations*

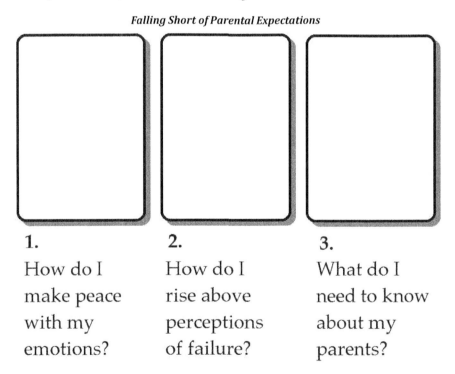

**1.**
How do I make peace with my emotions?

**2.**
How do I rise above perceptions of failure?

**3.**
What do I need to know about my parents?

After this session, return to the preceding divinatory reading and deep-dive into the messages of each card, but for now, gaze upon the three cards and free-write your impressions below.

Let's talk about heartbreak. What is the first heartbreak that comes immediately to mind? I don't mean the first in your life chronologically. I mean if I push you to answer right now, what is the heartbreak that you would blurt out? Describe your deepest, darkest scar.

This heartbreak can be love, but it doesn't have to be. Perhaps someone close to you disappointed you in a profound, emotional way. Perhaps you were betrayed by someone you trusted. Perhaps it was a time you experienced tragedy or death. Let's talk about one event that, after the storm, left you broken.

What you wrote was what first came to your mind when the question of heartbreak was presented. That suggests residual injury that is still affecting you to this day. Ask yourself: "Why can't I let go of the hurt from that experience?" Free-write below.

Return to your tarot or oracle deck. Shuffle your deck and while you do so, reread what you wrote in the two earlier prompts. Then pull three cards into the spread below. Before you pull each card, focus on the specific question presented for that card position. Write in your divinatory results into the card diagram.

### *Letting Go of Heartbreak*

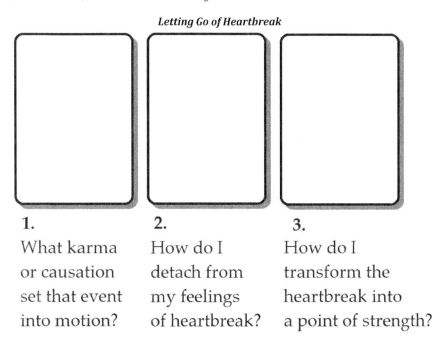

**1.**
What karma or causation set that event into motion?

**2.**
How do I detach from my feelings of heartbreak?

**3.**
How do I transform the heartbreak into a point of strength?

After this session, return to the preceding divinatory reading and deep-dive into the messages of each card, but for now, gaze upon the three cards and, relying upon the divinatory message of those cards, answer the following question: "What can I do going forward to be in service of others and to ensure that they need not suffer the way that I have?" What do the three cards tell you about how to turn heartbreak into productivity?

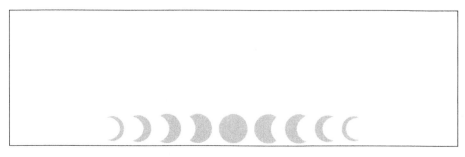

Turn over your deck and sift through it, face up, in search of one card that best represents who you want to be going forward, irrespective of your past. Note that card in the diagram below and in the space provided below, write out three resolutions for how you leave behind the past and think about your future, completing the sentence prompts.

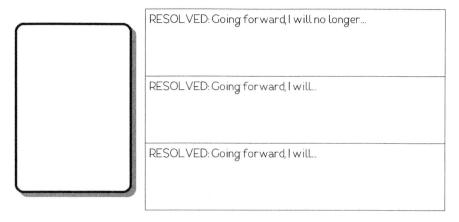

| RESOLVED: Going forward, I will no longer... |
| RESOLVED: Going forward, I will... |
| RESOLVED: Going forward, I will... |

Reflecting on the above card you have selected, think about what you would want to say to 11- or 13-year-old you. Think about what that child believes are the parental expectations to live up to. Think about your life path now, as an adult, filtered through the wisdom you have gained. What would you say to your child-self about your future, about living up to or not living up to other people's expectations, or when others do not live up to your expectations. What about when life does not meet your expectations and fantasies? Take time to write out your letter on the subsequent page.

*Letter to the Child You Once Were...*

After you've finished writing your letter to 11- or 13-year-old you, shuffle your deck, focus inward with concentrated emotion and feeling, releasing all of your emotions into the deck as you shuffle, feeling it all exit your hands and into the cards, and ask: "Give me a sign." Pull a card and note the card below, along with your first intuitive impressions.

Now pick up your bell (can also be tingsha cymbals or a singing bowl), exhale deeply, and with your exhale, envision all pain, anguish, heartbreak, and painful emotions leaving you through that exhale of breath and ring your bell. As you ring your bell, envision those dark emotions, on that exhale, scattering and disappearing from your vicinity. You feel the release, you are relaxed, and you feel at peace. Ring the bell once more to fully cleanse the area. You now feel some of what was in the shadow is now out in the light.

Recall the most memorable moment in your past when you displayed rage. This goes beyond anger. You were raging. You acted in a way toward another that, now in retrospect, you are just a bit ashamed of, because by raging, you know you let that person or that situation get under your skin. Note that moment below.

What exactly made you lose your temper and display rage? (What did someone do wrong, in your view, or what was unjust about that particular situation?)

In your view, why was the egregious conduct or situation so terrible that it would elicit rage from you?

Chances are you were taught that such conduct or this kind of situation is "not okay." Who taught you that this was "not okay"? (Here, don't say society, culture, community, or the government. Even if the matter is institutional, and in some way it probably is, someone, a *person, a human being* taught you this. Who was that human being?)

In other words, this person who taught you such conduct or situation was "not okay" was someone you admired, someone whose code of conduct and beliefs mattered to you, that you may have even adopted for yourself. This egregious conduct or situation offended you because if the egregious actors were allowed to get away with what was done, what was "not okay," then they in effect undermine the authority and power of this person you so admire. That's really what's not okay, isn't it? These egregious actors are undermining the authority and power of this person whose code and beliefs you've learned from.

Your conscious mind may know it's irrational, but some deep primal part of you wants everyone to follow the code and beliefs of this person you admire, mostly because you follow that code and those beliefs. Anyone and any situation that undermines that is going to trigger your hostility because they are undermining your power. You raged in that moment because the egregious actors undermined your code and beliefs, and your power.

Shuffle your deck while focusing on this question: What important lesson is there to learn about yourself from that event? Then draw a card. Note your results and impressions.

One final divinatory reading for yourself before we move on to the next section: shuffle the deck and draw two cards. Before drawing each card, shuffle and focus on the question presented, then pull the card.

**1.**
When my code and beliefs are undermined in the future, instead of giving in to rage, what must I focus on?

**2.**
What must I know and be always mindful of with regard to my personal temper?

Note any significant impressions you want to remember below.

Before moving on, take a moment to relax. Sit straight and tall in your seat. Imagine a string running down your spine and someone from up above, at the crown of your head, pulls on that string. Close your eyes and concentrate on your breath. Focus on 7 counts while you inhale, hold your breath for a moment, and then exhale 15 counts. Repeat 7 counts inhale, hold, and 15 counts exhale several more times. Then smile, open your eyes, and proceed.

Identify three attributes, circumstances, or matters that you feel are lacking or dysfunctional in your life right now. Summarize them in short form below.

| 1. | 2. | 3. |
|---|---|---|
| | | |

Now let's address each one separately. We'll start with the first one you noted above as "1." Each one of the three will be delved into in turn. Start by rewriting the first attribute, circumstance, or matter that you feel is lacking or dysfunctional in your life right now, in the present, into the space provided after "1." Then follow the prompts through the sub-questions for "1." Repeat the approach for "2." and then finally "3."

The prompts through each of the three points begin on the subsequent page.

| 1. |
|---|
| **It makes me** ---------------------------------------------------------------- |
| *Input emotion(s) [adjectives].* |
| *Check one of the boxes.* <br> **to feel that I** ☐ **lack** ☐ **fail at** |
| |
| *Complete the sentence with what you feel you lack or fail at.* |
| **However, that which I perceive to be lacking or failing is <u>illusory</u>.** |
| **Behind the feelings of inadequacy is the superficial and materialistic desire for** |
| |
| *Complete the sentence.* |

Pick up your tarot or oracle deck. Shuffle your deck and while you do so, reflect on the pain you feel from that lacking or failure. Also reflect on why that pain is illusory and the very superficial or materialistic desire that is actually fueling your feelings of inadequacy. As you pull each card into the spread noted below, focus on the specific question presented for that card position. Write in your divinatory results into the card diagram.

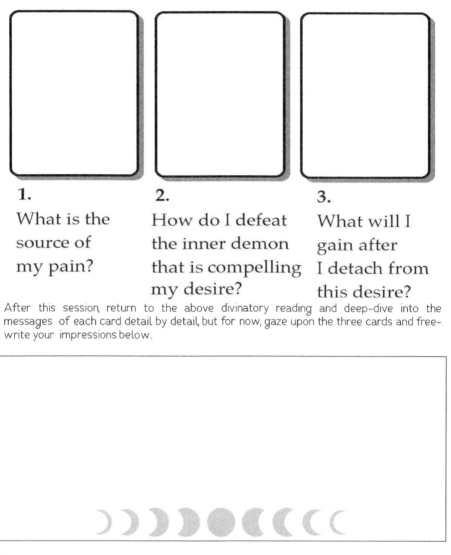

**1.**

What is the
source of
my pain?

**2.**

How do I defeat
the inner demon
that is compelling
my desire?

**3.**

What will I
gain after
I detach from
this desire?

After this session, return to the above divinatory reading and deep-dive into the messages of each card detail by detail, but for now, gaze upon the three cards and free-write your impressions below.

You may not have it all, but you are endowed with blessings that others have not been endowed with, that others lack. You have under your belt achievements that others have failed at. Turn the cards face up and sift through the deck to identify one card that represents a blessing in your life that you are proud of and note it in the diagram below. Then complete the sentences below by following the prompts. For the final prompt on

How you might optimize your blessing, think about how you can contribute to the greater good or how you can be of service to benefit another by utilizing your blessing.

| | I am blessed because... |
| --- | --- |
| | |
| | This blessing is a weapon of Light I use to defeat the Darkness that my shadow sense of lacking or failing has created. This blessing is the Light that conquers the Dark. |
| | I will optimize my blessing by... |
| | |

*Optional.* From the earlier prompt, "It makes me feel_____to feel that I lack (*or*) fail at _____," write out that emotion after "feel" onto a scrap sheet of paper. Fold it three times and as you fold it, envision all bottled feelings of inadequacy and that emotion surging out of your fingertips and into the paper. When you finish folding, you will feel a sense of release. Then burn the scrap of paper in the flame of your pillar candle. The light of the flame dissipates the shadow.

## 2.

| It makes me | ------------------------------------------------------------------------------------------------- |
| --- | --- |
| | *Input emotion(s) [adjectives].* |

*Check one of the boxes.*

to feel that I ☐ lack ☐ fail at

*Complete the sentence with what you feel you lack or fail at.*

**However, that which I perceive to be lacking or failing is <u>illusory</u>.**

**Behind the feelings of inadequacy is the superficial and materialistic desire for**

*Complete the sentence.*

Pick up your tarot or oracle deck. Shuffle your deck and while you do so, reflect on the pain you feel from that lacking or failure. Also reflect on why that pain is illusory and the very superficial or materialistic desire that is actually fueling your feelings of inadequacy.

As you pull each card into the spread noted below, focus on the specific question presented for that card position. Write in your divinatory results into the card diagram.

| | | |
|---|---|---|
| **1.** | **2.** | **3.** |
| What is the source of my pain? | How do I defeat the inner demon that is compelling my desire? | What will I gain after I detach from this desire? |

After this session, return to the above divinatory reading and deep-dive into the messages of each card detail by detail, but for now, gaze upon the three cards and free-write your impressions below.

)))) ● (((( (

You may not have it all, but you are endowed with blessings that others have not been endowed with, that others lack. You have under your belt achievements that others have failed at. Turn the cards face up and sift through the deck to identify one card that represents a blessing in your life that you are proud of and note it in the diagram below. Then complete the sentences below by following the prompts. For the final prompt on how you might optimize your blessing, think about how you can contribute to the greater good or how you can be of service to benefit another by utilizing your blessing.

I am blessed because...

This blessing is a weapon of Light I use to defeat the Darkness that my shadow sense of lacking or failing has created. This blessing is the Light that conquers the Dark.

I will optimize my blessing by...

*Optional.* From the earlier prompt, "It makes me feel_____to feel that I lack (or) fail at _____," write out that emotion after "feel" onto a scrap sheet of paper. Fold it three times and as you fold it, envision all bottled feelings of inadequacy and that emotion surging out of your fingertips and into the paper. When you finish folding, you will feel a sense of release. Then burn the scrap of paper in the flame of your pillar candle. The light of the flame dissipates the shadow.

| 3. |
|---|
| **It makes me** _____ |
| *Input emotion(s) [adjectives].* |
| *Check one of the boxes.* |
| **to feel that I** ☐ **lack** ☐ **fail at** |
| |
| *Complete the sentence with what you feel you lack or fail at.* |
| **However, that which I perceive to be lacking or failing is <u>illusory</u>.** |
| **Behind the feelings of inadequacy is the superficial and materialistic desire for** |
| |
| *Complete the sentence.* |

Pick up your tarot or oracle deck. Shuffle your deck and while you do so, reflect on the pain you feel from that lacking or failure. Also reflect on why that pain is illusory and the very superficial or materialistic desire that is actually fueling your feelings of inadequacy. As you pull each card into the spread noted below, focus on the specific question presented for that card position. Write in your divinatory results into the card diagram.

**1.**

What is the source of my pain?

**2.**

How do I defeat the inner demon that is compelling my desire?

**3.**

What will I gain after I detach from this desire?

After this session, return to the above divinatory reading and deep-dive into the messages of each card detail by detail, but for now, gaze upon the three cards and free-write your impressions below.

You may not have it all, but you are endowed with blessings that others have not been endowed with, that others lack. You have under your belt achievements that others have failed at. Turn the cards face up and sift through the deck to identify one card that represents a blessing in your life that you are proud of and note it in the diagram below. Then complete the sentences below by following the prompts. For the final prompt on how you might optimize your blessing, think about how you can contribute to the greater good or how you can be of service to benefit another by utilizing your blessing.

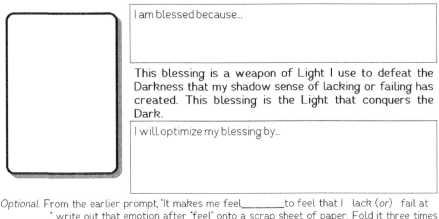

I am blessed because...

This blessing is a weapon of Light I use to defeat the Darkness that my shadow sense of lacking or failing has created. This blessing is the Light that conquers the Dark.

I will optimize my blessing by...

*Optional.* From the earlier prompt, "It makes me feel_____to feel that I lack (*or*) fail at _____," write out that emotion after "feel" onto a scrap sheet of paper. Fold it three times and as you fold it, envision all bottled feelings of inadequacy and that emotion surging out of your fingertips and into the paper. When you finish folding, you will feel a sense of release. Then burn the scrap of paper in the flame of your pillar candle. The light of the flame dissipates the shadow.

For the next step, you'll need extra paper. On a scrap sheet of paper, write out a desire or impulse that you feel ashamed for having. You'd say immediately that this is, of course, something you would *never* act out. You *know better* than that.

Yet if you're being honest with yourself, that desire or impulse is there nonetheless. You don't have to write it out explicitly in this workbook. Instead, write it on a scrap sheet of paper. If you're not sure what is meant by "desire or impulse," think about sins as many religions have dictated.

Think about what would be criminal or immoral. What desire or impulse do you have that society would deem either criminal or immoral? That's what you write on that scrap of paper.

Now shuffle your deck and draw three cards, while focusing on what you've written on that scrap of paper. Also, as you draw each card into the spread, present the question noted for each card and ask it of your cards (i.e., of your Higher Self or of Divinity). Note your card results in the subsequent card diagram.

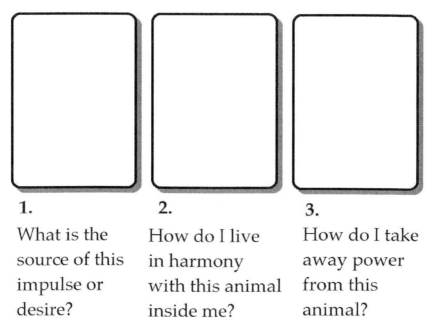

**1.**

What is the source of this impulse or desire?

**2.**

How do I live in harmony with this animal inside me?

**3.**

How do I take away power from this animal?

At your option, document any notes from the reading below.

Next, fold that scrap of paper three times and as you fold, recite the following: "I live in harmony with my inner beast, because I control you and I take away your power. I expose you to the Light and with that Light, your power is exorcised." Then feed the folded paper to the flame of your pillar candle and watch it burn. Ring the bell once to scatter any residual unwanted energies in the air.

Often when we dislike someone with intensity, it is because that person represents traits we secretly wish we could embody ourselves, but we do not because we "know better." We know that based on social constrictions, we cannot act that way. It wouldn't be "right." So when we see someone else acting in ways we *want* to act but don't because we "know better," we project. We feel deep dislike for that person because they are doing something "wrong," but that "wrong" thing is something we secretly wish we could do ourselves. That person gets to release out into the open what we ourselves have to repress. Therefore we project and what comes out is a deep, intense dislike for that person.

Now, name someone you dislike immensely. This person can be someone you know personally or a public figure, but it must be someone who causes you to have a visceral reaction, and a negative one. In the space below, explain what it is exactly you dislike about this person.

Then be honest with yourself. What is it about this person that you secretly wish you could be yourself, if there were no consequences to you being that way? Think about what *you're* repressing and therefore projecting dislike and even envy onto another.

Intense dislike for another is toxic to ourselves, which is why it is part of our shadow. That negative feeling obfuscates your higher calling and focus on your own path. Shuffle your deck and perform a three-card reading as noted below. As you draw each card, focus on the question prompted for that card position.

**1.**
How do I make peace with what I lack, which that person has?

**2.**
How do I quash the negativity I harbor toward this person?

**3.**
What will I gain or overcome after I neutralize my negativity?

Do a five-card cross reading for yourself. Draw the cards in the order and into the spread position noted below. Card 1 is where you are now. Card 2 is an innate gift or talent for you to develop and bring to the surface. Card 3 represents past influences. Card 4 is where you are headed, given present variables at play. Card 5 is a revelation, a spiritual message from the Divine, or from your Higher Self to your present consciousness. In the space provided below, note the cards drawn and your insights into the cards.

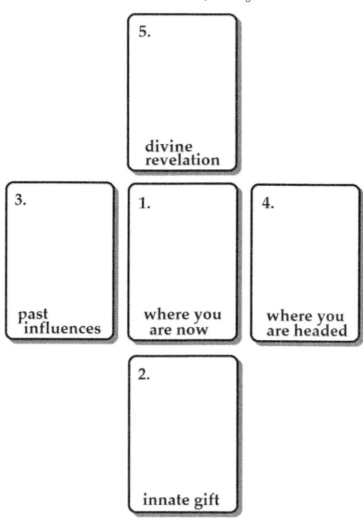

We often let our fears of what has yet to happen disable us. We allow our fears of the future to disempower our present. When you think about the next five years of your life path, what are you most afraid of? What is that *event* or terrifying *outcome* that you fear *could* happen, that you would rather not speak of or think of, that the mere utterance of gives you a sense of disempowerment? Utter it. Write it below. Face that fear head-on.

**You can prevent that outcome from ever happening to you.**

Pick up your deck. Shuffle and envision all your fears of that event or terrifying outcome intensifying within you and then surging through you, toward your hands, and out your fingertips into your cards. As you envision these fears, like an intense, concentrated current of energy being released into the cards, also state loud, "Transform my fears into a positive plan." Repeat that sentence, "**Transform my fears into a positive plan**" several times until you feel drained of energy. Then pull three cards and note the results below.

The three cards you pulled represent a three-step plan for how you can transform your fears and seize the power back from those fears. You will know the chronology, whether it is right to left or left to right for you. In the subsequent space provided, free-write on this three-step plan that the Divine or your Higher Self has revealed to you.

In the left column below, indicate the card you pulled that represents that particular step in the chronology. Then in the right column, interpret that card as insights into how you can transform your fears into an empowering plan forward.

| | |
|---|---|
| *First Card* \| **Step One** | |
| *Second Card* \| **Step Two** | |
| *Third Card* \| **Step Three** | |

Notwithstanding your solid empowerment plan forward that will avert the danger of your fears, know this: **Your fear is __illusory__.** Thus, knowing that, complete the below sentence.

| **Behind the fear is attachment and bondage to** |
|---|
| |
| *Complete the sentence.* |

Pick up and shuffle your deck. While you do so, recite the passage below. Recite it aloud.

That bondage is created by my ego and its desires for materialistic and superficial forms of happiness. If I defer to my ego, then I give in to my fears and that bondage. Instead, I will defer to my Higher Self, to Divinity, and every step forward, I will be mindful of conduct and speech that is virtuous with my moral code. I will be mindful of the empowerment plan. All else I release to the Cosmos. What I cannot control was not intended for me to control, and when I defer to my Higher Self and not my ego, I can fully accept that Truth.

When you have finished reciting the passage, stop shuffling after you've recited the final word. Draw the top-most card in the deck and set it down. Then draw the bottom-most card in the deck and set it next to the first card, as indicated below.

**Top card in deck.**     **Bottom card in deck.**

The top card represents what is most likely to manifest in the immediate and upcoming stage of your life, i.e., the rest of this year and the next. The bottom card represents the most likely outcome to manifest five years from now.

Reflect on the two cards. What do they say about your fears of the future? If the energies prognosticate a positive outcome that shows your fears are unfounded, then write out what measures you will take each year, from Year 1 (represented by the top card in the deck) to Year 5 (the bottom card) to strive fearlessly for your goals and ambitions. If, however, the energies prognosticate a likelihood that the terrifying outcome you fear most could happen, then revisit the three-card reading and that three step plan revealed to you through divination. Write out your resolutions and what you will do each year for the next five years to stay the course of that empowerment plan.

| | |
|---|---|
| Year 1 | |
| Year 2 | |
| Year 3 | |
| Year 4 | |
| Year 5 | |

Now think about what you have. What are three blessings you have in your life right now that you are afraid of losing? These blessings can be your beauty, your physical health, your business, career success, your wealth, someone you love, your marriage, your child, a particular talent or ability, or a particular physical or non-physical attribute of yours. Note three of such blessings in the space below.

| 1. | 2. | 3. |
|----|----|----|
|    |    |    |

Now let's address each one in turn. For each numbered box, transfer over the blessing you noted above into the given space and continue the line of prompts and inquiry for that particular blessing or attachment. We will begin with the first one.

| 1. |
|----|
|    |

*Blessing or current attachment you are afraid of losing.*

Why is this something you are afraid of losing? Specifically, how would the loss affect *you*?

|  |
|--|
|  |

How does having this blessing in your life right now serve your ego?

|  |
|--|
|  |

In what way is your attachment superficial or materialistic? [Refrain from being defensive. If you face the truth, you'll accept that there is *some* way in which this blessing is bondage.]

|  |
|--|
|  |

Page 76

Shuffle your tarot or oracle deck and as you do, ask yourself, "How do I overcome my fear of losing..." and complete the sentence with what it is specifically you've noted above in 1. Then draw a single card and free-write your impressions in the space provided below.

Recall the second blessing or attachment in your life right now that you fear losing. Follow the prompts below.

**2.**

*Blessing or current attachment you are afraid of losing.*

Why is this something you are afraid of losing? Specifically, how would the loss affect *you*?

How does having this blessing in your life right now serve your ego?

In what way is your attachment superficial or materialistic?

Shuffle your tarot or oracle deck and as you do, ask yourself, "How do I overcome my fear of losing..." and complete the sentence with what it is specifically you've noted above in 2. Then draw a single card and free-write your impressions in the space provided below.

Finally, the third blessing in your life right now you are attached to:

**3.**

*Blessing or current attachment you are afraid of losing.*

Why is this something you are afraid of losing? Specifically, how would the loss affect *you*?

How does having this blessing in your life right now serve your ego?

In what way is your attachment superficial or materialistic?

Shuffle your tarot or oracle deck and as you do, ask yourself, "How do I overcome my fear of losing..." and complete the sentence with what it is specifically you've noted above in_. Then draw a single card and free-write your impressions in the space provided below.

Embedded in our shadow selves is the fear of not achieving what we most want to achieve. Think about the next ten years of your life path. What is that one aspiration you hope to achieve in the coming ten years, which if you do not achieve will cause regret?

What is the selfish reason for why you want to achieve that aspiration?

You believe you will regret it if you do not achieve your aspiration because the self-interested reason you noted for the aspiration is what you think you need to validate the worth of your life.

However, that sentiment is _illusory_. Your worth is not tethered to this aspiration.

Your worth comes from spiritual awakening and the relationship you establish with your Higher Self or the Divine. To strengthen that relationship, you dedicate yourself to service of a greater good. Right-hand path or left-hand path, to establish your self-worth, you have to become what is much greater than your physical self. Irrespective of personal gnosis, part of what establishes your sense of self-worth is feeling like the essence of you occupies space that is much larger and greater than the physical space that is you.

How do you achieve that? You may have convinced yourself that it will be through the manifestation of that particular aspiration of yours. Your subconscious believes that manifesting that particular aspiration will establish the essence of you as occupying space that will be much larger and greater than the physical body that is you.

So deconstruct your aspiration. There is an aspiration behind the aspiration. What is that aspiration behind your aspiration? How exactly would the achievement of your initial aspiration empower you to occupy space that is much larger and greater than you?

Know that so long as you achieve that aspiration behind that aspiration, whether you accomplish it through the initial aspiration or by other means, you will find fulfillment. That is why it is important to know the aspiration behind the aspiration.

Now defer to the Divine. Shuffle your deck and draw three cards into the spread illustrated in the subsequent diagram, following the questions prompted for each card position. Cards 2 and 3 are read as a pair.

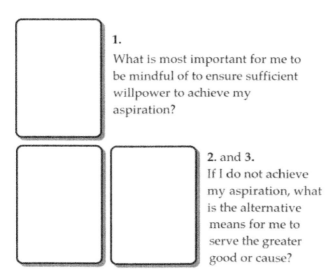

**1.**
What is most important for me to be mindful of to ensure sufficient willpower to achieve my aspiration?

**2. and 3.**
If I do not achieve my aspiration, what is the alternative means for me to serve the greater good or cause?

Remember: there are many paths to the same destination. Do not fear whether you will achieve your aspiration, though pursue that aspiration proactively. Focus on the present and what steps need to be taken in the present toward that goal. If you do not achieve that aspiration, know that there is an alternate route to still achieve what it is you ultimately want from that aspiration—validation for the worth of your life.

Below, free-write your impressions of the card reading.

Now pick up your bell, exhale deeply, and with your exhale, envision all of your disempowering fears leaving you through that exhale of breath. Then ring your bell. As you ring your bell, envision those dark emotions, on that exhale, scattering and dissipating from your vicinity. You feel the release, you are relaxed, and you feel at peace. Ring the bell once more to fully cleanse the area.

You now feel some of what was in the shadow is now out in the light.

In the cross reading you did for yourself earlier, one of the cards represented your innate gift. Sift through your deck and locate that card again. Pull it out of the deck and set it on your work space. Note the card in the space below for "(2. Innate Gift)." In the cell to its right, note in what ways you are aware of this innate gift.

| (2. Innate Gift) | |
|---|---|
| | |

Shuffle the rest of the deck and while you do so, fix your gaze on the innate gift card. Shuffling, before you draw each of the three cards below, ask the noted question for each card position, shuffle, and then draw your card. Note your results in the diagram.

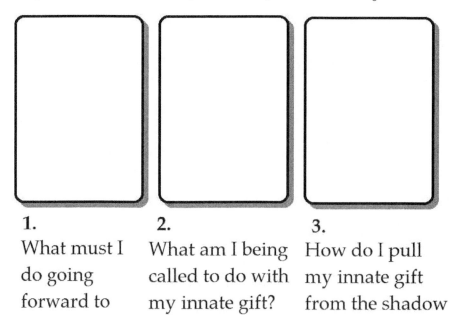

**1.**
What must I do going forward to advance my gift?

**2.**
What am I being called to do with my innate gift?

**3.**
How do I pull my innate gift from the shadow into the light?

Following the counsel of the three cards, make plans. Think about what you seek to overcome your inner feelings of inadequacy. You will do this by utilizing your innate gift and being productive through use of that gift. Solidify a concrete plan for what you

Page 82

seek to accomplish in the next year toward utilizing your gift in a way that will be productive. In the below space, write out at least five resolutions on how you will develop, advance, or utilize your innate gift in the coming year.

| RESOLVED: | |
|---|---|
| RESOLVED: | |
| RESOLVED: | |
| RESOLVED: | |
| RESOLVED: | |

*Practice Tip.* If you have a daily planner or journal, integrate your resolutions into a personal document that you will see day to day and be consistently reminded of.

### CLOSING THE SESSION

After you have completed this self-guided workbook, take a moment to review your responses and reading results, from the first page to the last. Direct your gaze at the flame of the burning pillar candle. Observe the new formation of wax around the candle, which has occurred during the time you went through this session. Like the candle, you are still the same, but now you have a reformed consciousness.

Recite aloud: "There is no weight to my shadow. It does not hold me down. I release my pain into the light and by doing so, free the innate gift with which I will manifest my life purpose and higher calling."

Solidify within you all the pain, regrets, feelings of inadequacy, disappointments at your own failures and as you exhale firmly to blow out the candle, envision all that darkness and toxic negativity exit from you with the exhale. When the flame goes out, that light takes with it all the toxic negativity you've released out of yourself and as the smoke dissipates, your bondages, tethers, and attachments dissipate with it. Ring the bell one final time to scatter completely all residual toxic energies. You now feel calm and relaxed.

Make a note to revisit the results of your session three months from now. If some facets of the divinatory readings you performed during the session don't make sense in the moment, trust the process, because later in time when you revisit the reading, more pieces will fall into place and you can gain new insights.

For record-keeping purposes, note the tarot or oracle deck you used for your session.

|  |
| --- |
| *Deck used for this self-guided shadow work session.* |

Date session was conducted:

|  |
| --- |

Calculate three months from the session date and note below. Also write down the anniversary date. You'll want to revisit the reading yet again one year from now.

|  |  |
| --- | --- |
| *Three Months from Date of Session* | *One Year from Date of Session* |

### THREE MONTH REVIEW

After three months, review your session notes and document any new insights gained from the review. Note any new impressions below.

|  |
| --- |

# ONE YEAR REVIEW

After one year, reflect on your actions that year and whether you've stayed the course of your own resolutions. In the space below, note impressions and any progress you've made in the year on working through shadows of the present.

If any remain incomplete, enter them as resolutions tasked for the coming year. After your one-year review, what else remains to be done? Note your five resolutions for the next year. Start by carrying over all incomplete resolutions from the previous year. If all five remain incomplete, then the upcoming year will be focused on those same five resolutions. If only three were complete, then carry over the two remaining resolutions and add three new ones.

| RESOLVED: | |
|-----------|---|
| RESOLVED: | |
| RESOLVED: | |
| RESOLVED: | |
| RESOLVED: | |

# TAKEAWAY

Carl Jung, a physician and psychologist, pioneered shadow work. It delves into aspects of yourself that you have shunned or suppressed.

Typically, a shadow begins to form throughout early infancy, when we are taught that certain acts are wrong. Shadow work proponents assert that it may aid in the healing of generational trauma, enable individuals to reconsider the signals they send their children, manage with emotions more constructively, and feel more entire.

While shadow work is often done in therapy, there are certain exercises that you may practice alone.

Some of the most valuable lessons we will learn in this life will come from confronting the aspects of ourselves that we conceal. Because when we are able to bring our shadows to the surface, heal them, and incorporate them into our life, we exponentially progress. After all, it was Jung who stated, "There is no path to consciousness that is not accompanied by sorrow."

Printed in Great Britain
by Amazon